A modern appr

Reading and w e
natural activity e
next most impo s
designed to stimulate and interest him and to give daily practice at the right level.

Educational experts from five Caribbean countries co-operated with the author to design and produce this Ladybird Sunstart Reading Scheme. Their work has been influenced by (a) the widely accepted piece of research ***Key Words to Literacy***[1], adapted here for tropical countries. This word list has been used to accelerate learning in the early stages. (b) The work of Dr Dennis Craig[2] of The School of Education, U.W.I., and other specialists who carried out research in areas where the English language is being taught to young children whose natural speech on entering school is a patois or dialect varying considerably from Standard English.

1 *Key Words to Literacy*, by J McNally and W Murray, which was published by the Schoolmaster Publishing Co. Ltd., England.

2 *An Experiment in Teaching English*, by Dennis R Craig, which was published by the Caribbean Universities Press, also Torch (vol. 22, No.2), Journal of the Ministry of Education, Jamaica.

The Ladybird Sunstart Reading Scheme consists of six books and three workbooks. These are graded and written with a controlled vocabulary and plentiful repetition of the most used words in the English language. They are fully illustrated.

Book 1 ***Lucky dip*** (for beginners) is followed by book 2 ***On the beach***. ***Workbook A*** is parallel to these and covers the vocabulary of both books. The workbook reinforces the words learned in the readers, teaches handwriting and introduces phonic training.

Book 3 ***The kite*** and book 4 ***Animals, birds and fish*** follow books 1 and 2, and are supported by ***Workbook B***. This reinforces the vocabulary of books 3 and 4 and again contains handwriting exercises and phonic training.

Book 5 ***I wish*** and book 6 ***Guess what?*** with ***Workbook C*** complete the scheme.

The illustrated handbook for parents and teachers is entitled ***A Guide to the Teaching of Reading***. The flash cards produced for Sunstart's parent scheme, ***The Ladybird Key Words Reading Scheme*** support the reading process.

Published by Ladybird Books Ltd
A Penguin Company
Penguin Books Ltd, 80 Strand, London WC2R 0RL, UK
Penguin Books Australia Ltd, 707 Collins Street, Melbourne, Victoria 3008, Australia
Penguin Group (NZ) Ltd. 67 Apollo Drive, Rosedale, North Shore 0632, New Zealand

027

Printed in China

Ladybird Sunstart

On the beach

BOOK 2

written by W. Murray
illustrated by Martin Aitchison

a girl

Joy

a boy

Ken

You see a girl.
She is Joy.

You see a boy.
He is Ken.

Joy and Ken
look at a man.
He is a big man.

new words

Joy Ken

Ken knows the man.
He likes him.

Joy knows him
and she likes him.

The man knows the girl
and the boy.

He likes Joy and Ken.

---

new words knows likes him

read

write

Joy can read and write.

She likes to write
in the sand.

She wants to write to Ken.

Joy writes to Ken
in the sand.

She says to him,
Look at that, Ken.
Can you read that?

new words read write sand

Look, Ken, I can write.
Joy

Ken sees Joy
write in the sand.

He wants to write.

He writes in the sand
and says to Joy,
Look at this, Joy.
Read this.
Can you read this?

new word

this

Joy,
This is
you.

Ken likes to play.
He wants to play
on the sand.

Come on, says Ken.
You come and play.
Please come and play.
This is for you.

---

new words play on

Ken.

This is for you, says Joy.
This water is for you.

They play on the sand.
They play in the water.

The man they know
is in the water.
Ken and Joy see him.

new words they water

fish

boat

The man wants to fish.
He has a boat.
He is in the boat.
It is on the water.

Ken and Joy can see him
in the boat.
It is a little boat.

new words fish has boat

Ken and Joy like to fish.
They look for fish
in the water.

Ken has one.
He has a little fish.

Come and look at this,
he says to Joy.
I have one.

new word

have

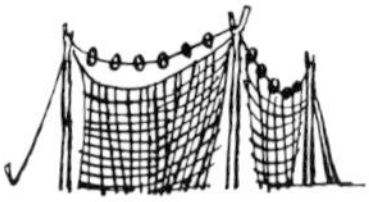

nets

men

You can see nets.
The nets are for the fish.
The men come for the nets.
They want to fish.

Ken and Joy look at
the men and the nets.

new words

nets men are

The boats are
on the water.

The men have the nets
in the boats.
Off they go.

The men go off
in the boats.
They go off to fish.

new words off go

The men go off to sea
in the boats.

They have the nets.

The nets go into the sea.
They go into the sea
for the fish.

The fish go into the nets.

new words

sea into

The men are on the beach.

They have the nets.

They pull the nets.

They pull the nets in.

Fish are in the nets,
big fish and little fish.

new words beach pull

Ken and Joy
are with the men
on the beach.

They see the men
with some fish.
Pull, pull, they say.
Pull the nets in.

Some birds see the fish.

new words some with

women

Some women are on the beach.

They see the men with fish.
The women want some fish.

They come to buy some.
They buy some fish
on the beach.

new words women buy

children

ball

The children are in the sea.
They like to play
in the water.

The children have a ball.
It is a big ball.

They see women
and children on the beach.

new words children ball

woman  Mummy

man  Daddy

I want the ball, says Ken.

You can have it, says Joy.

The children can see that
a man and a woman
are on the beach.

I see Mummy and Daddy,
says Joy.

new words woman Mummy Daddy

Yes, says Ken.
I see Mummy and Daddy.

The two children go to
Mummy and Daddy.

Joy sees that Mummy
has a bag.

Ken sees that Daddy
has a box.

new words   Yes   yes   bag

Can we eat, please,
says Ken.

Yes, we want to eat,
says Joy.

We all want to eat,
says Daddy.

Mummy and Daddy
and the two children
all eat on the beach.

new words

we eat all

Joy looks to see
what she can find
on the beach.

She looks on the sand.
She looks in the sea.

She has a bag.

Mummy is with Joy.
She looks to see what
she can find for Joy.

new words what find

Joy says to Ken,
Come and see
what you can find.

No, says Ken.
No, thank you.
I want to play with Daddy.

Ken has his ball.
He plays with his Daddy.

---

new words

No no his

The ball goes up.
It goes into a tree.

Ken goes up the tree
for the ball.
He likes to go up the tree.

Daddy looks up at him.

---

new words goes up

an orange

Look at me, Joy, says Ken.
Look at me, up this tree.
You come up the tree.

No, says Joy.
No, thank you.
I want an orange.

She sees that Mummy
has an orange.

new words
me an orange

Mummy has an orange
for Joy.
One for you, Joy, she says.

I want an orange,
says Ken.
One for me, please.

Yes, one for you,
says Mummy.
One for you, Ken.

no new words

Read the words with the help of the pictures.
Then cover the pictures and read the words.

---

1 **Ken plays with sand and water.**

2 **Some oranges are in this bag. She eats an orange. We all like oranges.**

3 **Has he a ball? No, he has a fish.**

4 **Off you go, she says to the bird.**

5 **The boy is on a box. Pull me up, he says.**

6 **Have you a bag, the woman says. Yes, says Mummy.**

7 **Daddy buys a ball for Ken.**

8 **He goes up the tree for his ball.**

9 **Joy looks on the beach to see what she can find.**

10 **The women know the men. They see the men go into the sea for the nets.**

11 **He reads and she writes.**

12 **The children see him go in the boat.**

All the 49 new words in this book are on this page.

1
2
3
4
5
6
7
8
9
11
12

Words new to the series used in this book

Cover: on beach (see below)

Page		Page	
4	Joy Ken	28	some with
6	knows likes him	30	women buy
8	read write sand	32	children ball
10	this	34	woman Mummy Daddy
12	play on	36	yes bag
14	they water	38	we eat all
16	fish has boat	40	what find
18	have	42	No his
20	nets men are	44	goes up
22	off go	46	me an orange
24	sea into	48	–
26	beach pull	50	–

Total number of words 49